CW00504434

ISBN-13: 978-1500680657

ISBN-10: 1500680656

First published 2014 by:
Bustle & Sew
Coombe Leigh
Chillington
Kingsbridge
Devon TQ7 2LE
UK

www.bustleandsew.com

Welcome ......

There's a wonderful feeling of freedom in the air at the beginning of August - the month for holidays, and the chance to escape your everyday routine - if only for a short time. Around now I always succumb to the illusion that the warm weather, long dreamy days in the sunshine and the sense of summer stretching ahead will continue forever.

I've tried to bring you a little summer sunshine in this issue's projects too, with the Flanders Poppies cushion - remembering the anniversary of World War 1 - Emily and Arthur, the two little rabbits and True Beauty Peacock. You'll also discover a delightful little embroidered loveheart - the perfect project to pop in your bag (could this be the Summer Birdie Bag?) and take around and about with you for some outside stitching as you make the most of the long warm summer days still to come.

You may notice a few changes on the magazine pages this month - and there'll be more to come in future issues with exciting times ahead as Rosie joins me here at Bustle & Sew. We have all kinds of nice things planned for future issues, as well as a complete overhaul of the Bustle & Sew website. But one thing that won't change is the Bustle & Sew projects - there'll still be loads to choose from in every issue, and next month will bring the first of this year's Christmas patterns.

The September issue is published on Thursday 28 August - but that's still a long way off - so be sure to make the most of all your stitching time this month, wherever you may be.

Helen xx

Taking a picnic to the beach? Why not add some fruity and herby ice cubes to your flask of drinks?
They're really easy to make and such an attractive treat. Just place a small piece of fruit - a raspberry
perhaps or a cube of watermelon and/or a sprig of mint in each section of an ice-cube tray, fill with
water and freeze. Using filtered water ensures your cubes will be deliciously clear. Consume within a
month - lovely!

Contents

SUMMER

August is the month for holidays and harvests - a busy time for those who work on farms and also in tourism. The hottest days of the year often fall in the month of August and are welcomed by farmers as they try to gather in the harvest. The last Monday in August is a public holiday in most of the UK and as the last of summer it's marked by various outdoor activities. The naval dockyards of Portsmouth and Plymouth are opened to the public in alternate years for Navy Days, whilst in London thousands of people take to the streets for the Notting Hill Carnival which features colourful processions, elaborate and extravagant costumes and the music of steel bands. It originated in the mid-1960s as a way of celebrating and maintaining the cultural traditions of the Caribbean migrants who live in and around the area.

August 1st sees the feast of Lammas, one of the four great pagan festivals of Britain. The festival of the Gule of August, as it was called, was probably a harvest festival and this tradition continued after the arrival of Christianity. Lammas was the time for country fairs, especially sheep fairs and other festivities, whilst in Ireland and Scotland, 1 August was Lughnasadh, a festival in honour of Lugh, the pagan god of light and wisdom.

Loaves were baked from the first corn of the harvest and either presented as offerings or eaten at the celebratory feast, which also included newly dug potatoes and fresh summer fruits.

In the summer of 1940, at the height of the Battle of Britain in the Second World War, Winston Churchill made his famous speech in the House of Commons including the phrase *"Never in the field of human conflict was so much owed by so many to so few"* referring to the pilots involved in prolonged conflict between the Royal Air Force and the German Luftwaffe, defeat in which could have resulted in Germany's invasion of the UK.

And finally, August 14 this year marks the centenary of the beginning of the First World War - a time to remember and reflect upon what we today owe to past generations and the sacrifices they made for us.

August comes, and though the harvest fields are nearly ripe and ready for the sickle, cheering the heart of man with the prospect of plenty that surrounds him, yet there are signs on every hand that summer is on the wane and that the time is fast approaching when she will take her departure.... But, far as summer has advanced, several of her beautiful flowers and curious plants may still be found in perfection in the water-courses, and beside the streams – pleasanter places to ramble along than the dusty and all but flowerless waysides in August.

Chambers Book of Days (1864)

True Beauty Peacock

We all know that true beauty is not a pretty face or slender figure, but is an inner light shining brightly from the heart and this little stitchery reminds us of this.

The peacock is composed of simple applique shapes, and is a great way to use up your scraps. The stitches used are chain stitch, back stitch, straight stitch and feather stitch.

Shown mounted in a 10" hoop.

You will need:

- 12" square medium weight non-stretchy cream or white fabric

- Assorted scraps of patterned cotton fabric for peacock tail

- 3 ½" x 2" dark blue cotton fabric for body

- Tiny scraps of golden yellow and pink felt

- Stranded cotton floss in pink, golden yellow, dark blue and one other colour that works well with your patterned fabrics for the tail.

- Bondaweb

- 10" hoop

Method:

- Transfer the design (actual size) onto the centre of your background fabric. Doing this will help you position the different peacock feathers accurately.

- Using the reversed template trace the peacock feathers onto the paper side of your Bondaweb. Allow a little extra at the top edge of each feather so it will sit beneath and be overlapped by the feather above it.

You may find it easiest to number the feathers as you go so you can easily position them correctly.

Cut a little extra along the top of each feather so the next will overlap

Crest and beak cut in one piece

- Fuse the paper feather shapes to the reverse of your printed cotton scraps and cut out using long strokes so your edges are nice and smooth, with no jagged snippy cuts. Use dressmakers shears and hold them steady in one hand, moving the fabric around with the other hand whilst cutting. You may need to practise this, but cutting this way gives much better results than trying to move the scissors around your shape.

- Peel off the paper backing and position shapes onto background fabric using the pattern lines as a guide. Start with the bottom feathers on each side, and work up towards the top, overlapping the feathers as you go, finishing off with the centre top feather that will overlap the feathers on either side.

- Cut and position the peacock body and pink felt heart in the same way. Press on reverse to make sure the pieces are firmly adhered to the background fabric.

- Secure the peacock body, heart, crest and beak to the background using small straight stitches placed at right-angles to the applique shapes. Use two strands of floss.

- With two strands of floss and the colour you chose to co-ordinate with your fabric scraps work feather stitch around the edges of the feathers. If you're not sure how to work feather stitch please see the next page. Use the same colour around all the feathers for a harmonious feel - don't be tempted to use different colours it will just look bitty.

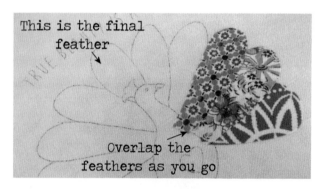

This is the final feather

Overlap the feathers as you go

- Now cut the crest and beak from golden yellow felt in the same way and position. I actually cut them in a single piece (see photograph) as this was much less fiddly than trying to position two tiny shapes - and neater beneath the blue fabric too.

- With two strands of floss and golden yellow thread work the peacock's feat in chain stitch. Add a couple of small stitches, or a French knot if you prefer, for his eye.

- Work the text in two strands of dark blue floss and back stitch except for the word "light" which is worked in one strand of floss and chain stitch.

- Your True Beauty embroidery is now complete.

Feather Stitch

Feather stitch is a lovely decorative stitch that's quick to sew and has lots of variations. Some old needlework books refer to it as plumage stitch as it was often used for working feathers in elaborate ecclesiastical and secular embroideries.

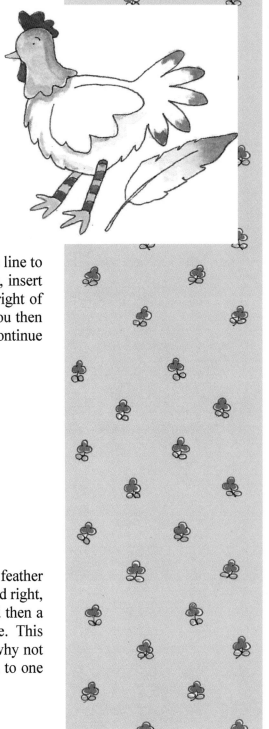

Bring your needle to the front of your fabric at the top of the line to be covered. Holding the thread down with your left thumb, insert your needle back into the fabric a little lower down to the right of the line and at an angle as shown in the diagram above. You then make a similar stitch on the left hand side of the line and continue working in this way.

Above is, I think, a delightfully pretty variation on ordinary feather stitch. Instead of making single stitches alternately to left and right, you work two or three consecutive stitches on one side, and then a similar number on the other side to create a pretty zigzag line. This makes for a light feathery effect in your embroidery - and why not experiment with making it quite irregular - say two stitches to one side, four to the next, three to the next and so on.

What makes us happy in August .....

Long, lazy sunny afternoons relaxing in the garden, strawberries and icecream, the sound of children playing ....

Lots of lovely village shows and fetes that showcase the best of all my friends' and neighbours' garden produce and handcrafted makes.

Courgettes, tomatoes and corn on the cob – produce picked fresh from the garden and put straight onto the barbeque – yum!

No need to switch on my worklamp - lovely light evenings and bright sunny mornings are the order of the day!

Patchwork pretties and crisp floral cottons .... The coolest of linens and frothy white lace..

Summer bunting - that I helped to make - cheerful colours against a clear blue sky at the village fete

Splashy waves, rockpools warm from the summer sun, driftwood bleached by salt and seawater, a small crab scuttling sideways to find a new hiding place amongst the pebbles, seaweed and starfish, two large black furry creatures bobbing up and down in a clear blue sea, then fish and chips from eaten from the paper – always tastes best – and a few chips for the Newfies too, sand between the toes and a good night's sleep dreaming of more summer days to come .... We like EVERYTHING about August – except that it has to end.... one day – but not yet!

Do MORE
of what makes
You
HAPPY

All Buttoned Up!

The humble button is an item we all take for granted these days, but did you know that the earliest date from the 6th century - well over a thousand years ago - when fitted clothing was introduced in the Middle East. Buttons made from small pieces of cloth sewn into a tight knob dating to the 14th century were among fragments of clothing discovered when the site of the Royal Wardrobe in the Blackfriars Bridge area of London was excavated in 1972, whilst writers of the time refer to gilt and silver gilt buttons being ordered for the royalty and nobility of the day.

In Tudor times, clothes for the rich became very colourful and elaborate, and were frequently decorated with numerous buttons made from precious metals and gemstone. Many of these buttons were later melted down and used either to make jewellery or to pay the debts of their owners. In contrast the clothes of the poorer people were simple and adorned with buttons made from leather or plain metal discs with a soldered band.

In the early 19th century the British button industry expanded rapidly following the Industrial Revolution and mechanisation. Birmingham was the centre of the industry supplying gilt buttons for the men and a huge variety of metal, shell, horn, ivory and even buttons crafted from nuts for ladies' clothing. In America the button-making industry was centred on the east coast with factories in Connecticut, Massachusetts and Pennsylvania, but once fresh-water shell had been discovered as a raw materials then factories sprang up all along the banks of the Mississippi.

The late 19th and early 20th centuries were possibly the peak of the decorative button industry. During this time the invention of paper patterns and the introduction of home sewing machines resulted in a boom in the haberdashery business. As in earlier times, buttons weren't used simply as fasteners, but also to decorate women's and children's clothing. This of course was the era of exploration and colonialisation and we shouldn't forget that the "clothing of the heathen" by Victorian missionaries also gave a boost to the button trade as utilitarian buttons were mass-produced in vegetable ivory, shell, linen to name but a few!

The years following the second world war were difficult times for British and European button makers because of the loss of premised due to war damage and also the shortage of labour and materials. They had to make do with what was available to them and it's not surprising that some rather strange buttons came onto the market including those made from plaster of paris, plastic-covered or plain wire, pulped paper, cork and even rabbit fur! American factories were less affected by the war, but were the first to feel the

impact of the introduction of the zipper. During the 1950s and 60s changes in fashions, the development of modern synthetic fabrics the zipper and even the tumble dryer resulted in widespread discontinuation of many button types in both Britain and America. I remember in my childhood being told that shell buttons would soon disappear forever - though these at least are now making a comeback. Indeed, buttons are enjoying something of a boom in popularity, with oodles of ideas to be found online for projects and makes using these amazingly versatile haberdashery items. For more inspiration check out these boards on Pinterest ….

http://uk.pinterest.com/barbara0101/button-crafts/
http://uk.pinterest.com/kirstyhelenyate/buttons/
http://uk.pinterest.com/tiggerhms/get-crafty-buttons/

Buttons are great in softie projects too - like this Running Hare from Bustle & Sew

A Jar for Buttons

Combine an inexpensive dumpy glass jar (mine was from Ikea Article Number 102.398.88) with a hoop, some applique and a little ingenuity and you have a lovely container for your button collection - or any other bits an bobs you might fancy storing within!

Great gift for a friend or to brighten up your own workspace.

You will need:

- 5" embroidery hoop

- 7" square background fabric, plain or patterned

- Scraps of fabric for applique

- 3 x 3/8" buttons - two for the owl's eyes and one for the word "buttons"

- Stranded cotton floss in golden yellow, two shades of green - light and dark, a dark colour for the text and colours to match the fabrics you've chosen for the owls'bodies, chests and the branch.

- Bondaweb

- Glue gun

- Emulsion or chalk paint to paint hoop (optional)

- Cotton tape to bind hoop inner

- 6" square felt

- 6" square medium weight cotton fabric - these last two are to back your design in the hoop.

- Temporary fabric marker pen.

Method:

- Transfer the design to the centre of your background fabric. It's not essential to transfer the lines for the applique shapes, but I find this is really helpful when I am positioning my pieces.

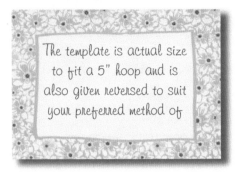

- Print out the REVERSE template and use this to trace the applique shapes onto the paper side of your Bondaweb.

- When you've traced your shapes, cut them out roughly and then fuse to the reverse of your fabric. Cut out carefully with long, smooth strokes of your scissors - I like to use dressmakers' shears as their long blades mean I can make long cuts, and not have lots of snips and jagged edges. Hold the scissors steady in one hand and move the fabric - don't try to move the fabric as you are cutting.

- Peel the paper backing from your shapes and position on the background fabric using the transferred pattern as a guide. Start with the branch, then the large owl body and after that the small owl body and the other smaller shapes.

- When you're happy with the positioning of your shapes fuse into place with a hot iron.

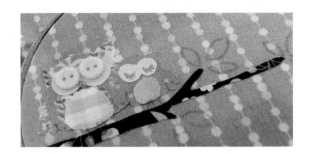

- With your temporary fabric marker pen draw in the baby owl's eyelashes

- Now add the embroidery. Secure around the edges of your applique shapes using two strands of matching floss and small straight stitches worked at right angles to the edges of the pieces.

- The feet and beaks are a few straight stitches worked in two strands of golden yellow.

- The baby owl's eyelashes are blanket stitch in the same dark coloured floss as you're using for the text. Stitch the adult owl's button eyes to the face using the same colour.

- The leaves are worked in satin stitch - stitch diagonally outwards from the centre to the edge, working the leaf in two halves.

- Work the text in back stitch using two strands of your dark coloured floss. Take small stitches around the curved parts of the letters so that the line is nice and smooth, paying particular attention to making sure your needle passes through back through the same hole after each stitch.

- Attach the button to the word "buttons" using the dark coloured floss.

- Remove temporary lines and press work on reverse. Your embroidery is now finished.

Mount in hoop:

- Remove the screw and paint the outer ring of the hoop with chalk paint or emulsion (optional) then reinsert the screw.

- Cut a circle of felt and a circle of backing fabric by drawing round the inside of your inner hoop. Put to one side for now.

- Your inner hoop should be larger (though not too much so) than the top of the jar. Wrap a layer of tape around it, overlapping slightly as you go, then test to see if it now fits fairly snuggly - though you will need to allow a little extra space for the embroidery fabric to be folded over it.. If the fit is too tight, then you'll need to wrap more sparsely, and if it's too loose then an extra layer of tape may be needed. When you're happy with how much tape is needed, secure one end of the tape to the hoop inner with your glue gun, then wrap around the inner hoop and secure again.

- Test your hoop fits nicely over the jar top before proceeding any further. (It should be slightly loose but not too much so).

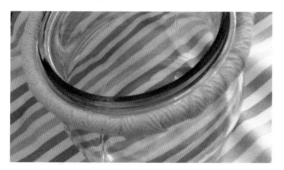

- Mount your embroidery in the hoop - you'll probably have to open the screw to its fullest extent to allow for both fabric and tape. Close the screw as tightly as you are able, then trim your fabric to 1" around the edge.

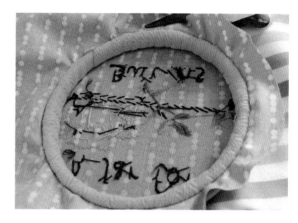

- Fold excess fabric towards the inside of the hoop and secure with your glue gun.

- Place the felt circle over the back of your embroidery and glue into place around the edge and then attach the backing fabric in the same way.

- Place hoop on top of jar and push down to secure over opening. Your button jar is now finished!

HERBS that Help you Sleep

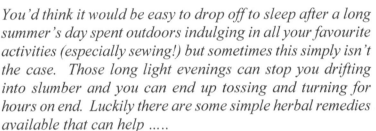

You'd think it would be easy to drop off to sleep after a long summer's day spent outdoors indulging in all your favourite activities (especially sewing!) but sometimes this simply isn't the case. Those long light evenings can stop you drifting into slumber and you can end up tossing and turning for hours on end. Luckily there are some simple herbal remedies available that can help .....

Camomile has been well established as a herbal aid to sleep since the time of the ancient Egyptians. It's native to Europe and northern Asia, and is now naturalised in the USA. Culpeper wrote that "the bathing with a decoction of chamomile taketh away the weariness, and easeth pain." He recommended the "flowers boiled in a posset drink."Camomile is a relaxant for the nervous system, soothing, calming and tranquilizing for restless or over-sensitive people. Its volatile oil with its delicious scent has the effect of relaxing muscles and aiding the digestion. Camomile tea is widely available commercially, or make your own by infusing 2 tablespoons of camomile flowers to 600 ml (approx 1 pint) of boiling water. Stand, covered, for 15 minutes, then strain and sweeten with honey.

Hops grow vigorously in northern temperate zones and are cultivated in Europe, the USA and Chile. Dried hop flowers, the female "cones" of the hop which are so strongly scented have been used to make "hop pillows" for the sleepless for generations. They help to sooth the highly strung, relax twitching or restless muscles and are a mild sedative. Make a cup of hop tea at bedtime, using the same method as camomile tea (above) for a good restful night's sleep.

Lavender is one of the best-known aromatic herbs. It's native to the Mediterranean, but is grown across the globe. It can be used to make a pillow in the same way as the hop pillow above adding, if you like, a few hops, some camomile flowers and lime blossoms. Sprinkle a few drops of lavender essential oil over the flowers before you sew up the pillow.

John Parkinson, herbalist and apothecary to King James I of England (VI of Scotland) in the early 17th century, describes the fragrance of lavender as "piercing the senses."

Lettuce has a very old reputation as a harmless herb to help and encourage sleep (another good reason to eat plenty of salads!). Its old-fashioned country names include "sleepwort". In the 18th century lettuces were grown for the white sap in their stems which contains lactucanum, which was used as a sedative up until the end of the 19th century. This substance was introduced into mainstream medicine in the 1770s and was known as "lettuce opium." It was even used to adulterate true opium, being a mild sedative and used before the days of anaesthetics for pain relief. So, if you want a good night's sleep, be sure to eat plenty of salad at bedtime, to ingest this natural sedative that sooths restlessness and muscle tension. Beatrix Potter's famous children's story of the Flopsy Bunnie falling asleep after munching their way through Mr McGregor's lettuces was based on scientific fact!

Valerian was used by early Arab physicians as a medicinal herb and still has a place in medicine today as a non-addictive tranquilizer, being found in many over the counter remedies. It reduces blood pressure, is useful in stress and insomnia and good for menopausal symptoms too. All heal, self heal and Blessed Herb are among its old country names.

Valerian should only be used on prescription since large does are inadvisable and it doesn't mix well with orthodox rugs. But it is powerfully sleep-inducing and soothes the over-sensitive, the nervous and worried and has been used to great effect in nervous exhaustion and anxiety states. Tincture of valerian was used to treat shell shock in the First World War.

In Flanders Fields

by

John McCrae

In Flanders fields the poppies blow
Between the crosses, row on row,
That mark our place, and in the sky
The larks, still bravely singing, fly
Scarce heard amid the guns below.

We are the Dead. Short days ago
We lived, felt dawn, saw sunset glow,
Loved and were loved, and now we lie,
In Flanders fields.

Take up our quarrel with the foe:
To you from falling hands we throw
The torch,; be yours to hold it high.
If ye break faith with us who die
We shall not sleep, though poppies grow
In Flanders fields

Lt Colonel John McCrae was a Canadian poet, physician and soldier, who acted as a surgeon during the second battle of Ypres. He died of pneumonia in 1918.

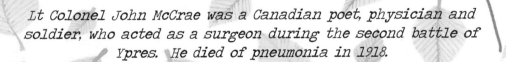

Flanders Poppies Cushion

As August 2014 sees the anniversary of the First World War - a conflict that affected all my grandparents, I wanted to create a design to commemorate the sacrifices their generation made. This poppies design is simple and feels very light and fresh - reflecting their hopes for a better future rather than looking backwards to the horrors of war.

Cushion measures 16" and has a simple envelope closure at the back

You will need:

- Two rectangles of medium weight blue dotty fabric each measuring 16 ½" x 12"

- One rectangle of medium weight blue dotty fabric measuring 16 ½" x 5 ½"

- One rectangle of medium weight cream fabric measuring 16 ½" x 11"

- 9" square red felt

- Scraps of dark red felt

- Stranded cotton floss in black (DMC310) and 3 shades of green - light, medium and dark

- Bondaweb

- Embroidery foot for your sewing machine.

- Temporary fabric marker pen.

- 16" cushion pad

Method:

- Transfer the design to the rectangle of cream fabric, centering it verticaly and with the ends of the stems ½" up from the bottom edge.

- Using the reversed design, trace the poppy shapes onto the paper side of your Bondaweb. When tracing the dark red petals at the backs of the flowers allow a little extra for them to be overlapped by the light red.

- Fuse the Bondaweb onto your felt and cut out the applique shapes with smooth strokes of your scissors (I like to use dressmaker's shears for long smooth cuts). Place to one side for now.

- Work poppy stems and buds using 2 strands of floss and your three shades of green. The poppy stems are worked in rows of chain stitch and the buds are also concentric rings of chain stitch - with a few stitches in a different green to add texture and interest.

- Now fuse the petals to the design with a hot iron using the transferred patter as a guide for positioning your shapes.

- Draw the lines for the petals onto the shapes with your temporary fabric marker pen.

- Fit the embroidery foot to your machine and with black thread in the needle and a paler colour in the bobbin (using black in both gives a very harsh, solid line) go around the edges of each flower twice, including the lines you drew for the petals. Don't be too neat, you are aiming for a sort of scribbled effect.

- Remove temporary fabric marker lines.

- Add centres to poppies - these are French knots worked in two strands of black floss.

- Press panel on reverse.

- Your applique is now finished.

- With a ¼" seam allowance join the smaller blue dotty rectangle to the bottom edge of your poppies applique. Finish seams by pinking, zig zagging or with a serger.

- Hem one long edge on each of the larger rectangles.

- Place your front panel face up on a clean flat surface, then your two back rectangles, aligning one long edge to the sides of the cushion and overlapping in the centre. Pin or tack then stitch around edge.

- Clip corners and finish seams, then turn right side out and insert pad.

- Your cushion is now finished.

The Surprising Health Benefits of Quilting

Jillyn Stevens PhD

You know that quilting makes you feel good, but now there's scientific evidence to back up what you've always suspected-not only does quilting make you happy, it's actually good for your health. Researchers at the University of Glasgow published their findings in the peer-reviewed Journal of Public Health after conducting qualitative research using a local quilting group as their source. The end result? "Quilting seemed to possess some distinct properties for enhancing well-being that would not be replicable through outdoor/physical activity." In other words, that's dry research speak for saying quilting gives you a workout you're not going to find in your local step class.

The biggest perk? When you're happy and doing something you love, your brain gets saturated with dopamine and serotonin, otherwise known as happy chemicals-especially when you're doing "meaningful work" using your hands. According to Kelly Lambert, PhD and a member of the neuroscience department at Randolph-Macon College, quilting complements these conditions perfectly.

Next on the health benefits list is a decrease in stress levels. Dr. Lambert says quilters "feel a sense of accomplishment that increases your 'reward chemicals' and decreases the chemicals related to stress or anxiety." Of course, lower stress levels are linked to a variety of good things from a lower risk of heart attack and stroke to lower body fat. In a time when stress levels are breaking through the roof for most people, who wouldn't benefit from a little cultivation of mindfulness?

If you're more into quantitative proof, a clinical psychologist published research in the Journal of the American Medical Association showing evidence that quilting leads to decreased blood pressure, heart rate and perspiration. Finally, according to Harvard neurologist Marie Pasinski, MD, quilting is a soother for the brain. The Glasgow research echoes these sentiments, with the participants saying that quilting was a (relatively) easy way to embrace creativity, and the use of different colours and textures gave them a "sense of wellbeing."

The Glasgow participants specifically cited, time and again, bright colours and how they elevated their moods-particularly during those dreary British winters. Most of the group also said there was something captivating about quilting and that they got into a flow, much like a runner's high. It's relaxing and at least for a little while, their anxieties were put on the back burner. However, quilting also requires problem solving skills, like when new patterns and shapes are required. From newbies to quilt masters, everyone said that at some point they always find a new challenge.

Finally, getting that tangible end result is a built-in reward that offers plenty of satisfaction and the feeling of achievement. During the social aspect of quilting as a group, the women said they felt inspired and all those compliments don't hurt when it comes to getting a self-esteem boost. Quilting is "uniquely good for you" concluded researchers-a sentiment that's obvious for quilters, but it's quite the rush to get a nod from the world of academe (kind of like nailing that tumbling blocks pattern on your first try).

Article Source: http://EzineArticles.com/?expert=Jillynn_Stevens,_Ph.D.,_MSW

Teacup Candelabra

My teacup candelabras were a favourite make for Rosie & Dan's wedding - and so easy too! Just look out for an inexpensive wooden or metal candelabra, remove the candle holders and paint with several layers of chalk paint. Rub down for that shabby chic look and preserve with some clear acrylic satin varnish. With Superglue Gel adhere vintage teacups where the candle holders were and fill with flowers of your choice - perfect!

Summer Birdie Bag

This pattern first appeared in Issue 7 of this magazine, back in 2011. It's a cute little bag that's really easy to make - and super fun to take around and about with you during the summer holidays, I thought it merited another outing.

I've dusted it off and carefully reviewed the instructions to bring it right up to date again.

Hope you like it!

Finished bag measures 14" wide x 13 ½ " deep

You will need:

- 32" x 12" cream canvas
- 44" x 12" spotty fabric for strap
- 26" x ¾ " wide twill tape or cotton ribbon
- 32" x 18" lining fabric
- 6" x 10" cotton fabric for interior pocket (optional)
- 44" x 1" strip of medium weight interfacing or 44" x 1" cotton twill tape
- Magnetic clasp (optional)
- Printer transfer paper or fabric suitable for printing directly onto to print the bunting flags with letters on them. If you don't have this then use scraps of floral fabric to make the bunting without letters

- 12" x 8" brown tweed, felt or other suitable fabric for branch
- 12" square green fabric for leaves
- Scraps of red and yellow fabric for bird
- Small button for bird's eye
- Bondaweb & fabric adhesie spray
- Invisible, black and light coloured thread
- Embroidery foot for sewing machine

Bird Applique:

- Using the template cut out two main bag pieces from your cream canvas. I have given the templates actual size, but they may come out differently depending on your printer. Just to check – the top edge of the templa te should measure 6 ¼" Please resize until this measurement is correct, otherwise your bag won't fit together properly!

- Trace the applique shapes onto the paper side of your Bondaweb. Make the bird's beak a little longer so it can be overlapped by the body fabric. Cut out roughly and fuse to reverse of fabrics. Cut out carefully with long smooth strokes, peel off the paper backing and position on one of your bag panels using the photograph as a guide. When you're happy with the positioning fuse into place with a hot iron protecting the fabric with a clean cloth if necessary.

- Print the bunting flags onto fabric or cut out the flags from floral fabric scraps. Position on design and hold in place with temporary fabric adhesive spray

- Fit the embroidery foot to your sewing machine and with black thread in the needle and a pale colour in the bobbin applique all your shapes to the front bag panel. Go around each shape twice, not too neatly for a sort of scribbled effect. You're using two different coloured threads to avoid a harsh solid line that isn't very attractive. Stitch up and down the centre of the leaves for the stalks, extending the stalks to the tips of the twigs so the leaves are attached.

- Applique the little bird in the same way – but only stitch once around his beak. Give him some little machine-stitched legs and claws.

- Apply and secure your bunting flags. Change the needle thread to cream and secure them around the edges with a medium zig-zag stitch.

Now change back to black in the needle (sorry, I know it's fiddly) and run two lines of stitching along the top of the bunting to represent the tape it hangs from. Make sure it looks loopy – as though it were secured to the branch and pulled downwards by the weight of the flags.

- Sew the button in place for the bird's eye. Your applique panel is now finished.

Assemble your bag: Interior

Seam allowance is ¼" throughout.

- Cut 2 main pieces in lining fabric

- Cut your spotty fabric as follows:

  4   pieces measuring 13 ½" x 4 ½" and

  1   piece measuring 44" x 5"

- Join the darts at the bottom corners of the bag main pieces (both interior and lining) matching A to A at the corners.

This picture is the exterior, but the process is exactly the same for the interior.

- If making interior pocket, take the pocket fabric and turn one short edge twice towards the reverse and stitch.

- With right sides facing, fold so that the unfinished edge is approximately ½" up from the hemmed edge.

- Stitch sides and turn right side out (see photograph). Press lightly.

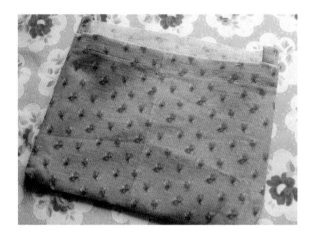

- Take one main lining piece and one spotty piece and place right sides together matching the top of the main piece to the long edge of the lining piece. Insert the pocket raw edge into the middle, with the pocket facing out from the main piece.

- Machine stitch together along top of main piece spotty and main pieces together along top of main piece including top edge of pocket.

- Join another rectangle of spotty fabric to the other piece of bag lining in the same way.

- Place the two lining panels right sides together and stitch around edge, leaving a 6" gap at the bottom for turning through. Clip curves.

- Insert magnetic clasp at centre of the dotty fabric and 2" down from top edge (if using)

Exterior:

- Join the spotty rectangles to the top edges of the bag main pieces in the same way. Top stitch the twill ribbon over the join between the two pieces of fabric.

- With right sides together join the front and back panels around the outer edge (leave the top edge open)

- To make the handle take your long piece of dotty fabric and fold sides to centre as shown in the picture below. Press.

- Position your twill tape or strip of interfacing down the middle of your strip and fold the sides cross enclosing it.

- Top stitch down sides of handle to keep everything in place.

- Turn the bag exterior right side out and place inside the exterior, lining up the top edges. The right sides of the interior and exterior should be together, ie the interior is wrong side out with the right side out exterior inside it.

- Position bag strap lining it up with the side seams. Pin or tack everything in place, and when you are happy machine stitch around the top of the bag. It's a good idea to run over the strap ends a couple of times for extra strength.

- Turn the bag right side out through the gap in the bottom of the lining and topstitch the gap closed. Push the lining down inside the bag and press top and side seams.

- Top stitch around the top edge of the bag ¼" or less from the edge. This gives you a nice neat firm finish and holds everything in place.

- Your bag is now finished.

A Little History of American Quilting

Part One: The Early Years

Traditional American quilts are comprised of three layers - the patchwork or pieced top, the batting or wadding - the layer that give the quilt warmth and substance and finally the backing fabric. These are held together by the process of quilting - the technique of joining layers of fabric with stitches.

I'm sure that as long as man has worn clothes, then women have been busy patching them - but did you know that the processes of piecing and quilting actually appear in recorded history as early as the ancient Egyptians? There are descriptions of various items, such as bedding and sails pieced together from different textiles and skins as early as 1,000 BC!

During the Crusades the European soldiers learned from North Africans that quilted clothing could offer some protection against wounds, as well as providing a comfortable underlayer for chain mail or armour if they were lucky enough to have any. The concept of quilting quickly caught on and so winter garments and bedclothes began to be quilted, with the fashion for quilted garments peaking in Spain during the late 16th century when it was the fashion (if you were rich enough of

course) to smother your clothing so heavily with jewels (and buttons too) that a single layer of fabric simply wasn't able to support the weight.

Back in England, almost everyone knows that William Shakespeare left his wife their second best bed and furnishings - which would have comprised a whole set of matching quilts, hangings and so on - which she'd probably stitched herself anyway! It seems likely that piecework was also being done in Europe at this time and there is still debate as to whether piecework travelled from England and Holland to the New World or the opposite way around. Whichever way it went, the early history of the American patchwork quilt follows quite naturally the history of the earliest Americans themselves.

The earliest colonists arrived on the east coast believing they'd discovered an earthly paradise, but sadly this proved not to be the case and before the first spring arrived more than half were dead of starvation and pneumonia. The colonies were undersupplied and unprepared in the early years and desperately improvised ways to repair or

replace what they'd brought with them and invent things they'd never anticipated needing.

From the indigenous population the colonists learned useful survival skills, whilst their country of origin simply gave them the Navigation Acts, laws designed to protect England's trade monopolies, particularly in textiles. It became illegal for the colonists to manufacture their own textiles, or to buy them from any country except England. In fact it was illegal for anyone trained in textile manufacture to emigrate to America!

During these early years, life was very hard for the colonists as they struggled to establish a foothold in their new country. It was at this time that the crazy quilt was invented.

A lovely decorative example is shown in the photo above, but these earliest ones would not have been so lovely, being made from clothes and bedclothes that had already been used till they fell apart, cut down for the children and used again until finally they were cut up to salvage every usable scrap and sewn together to serve as bedding. These early quilts would have been filled with whatever their makers had to hand - dried leaves, scraps and rags,

shredded paper and in many ways they symbolise the hardship and frustration of the early years in New England.

However, by the late 17th century the colonies had passed laws in defiance of the Navigation Acts requiring every woman and child to spin a certain amount of flax every day. Sheep were being raise and so quilts could now be stuffed with fleece which must have been warmer, though probably a lot smellier than rags or paper! Best of all cottons began to be exported to both England and America by the East India company - though the British vested interests fought back. By the turn of the century importing cotton goods was made illegal in England and the colonies, and by 1729 it was illegal even to wear cotton! These laws however were impossible to enforce and were so flagrantly violated that they were repealed and in the colonies were replaced with a new set of taxes that meant a length of fabric cost around four times as much as it did in England, whilst anyone using a spinning wheel or loom at home had to pay an additional tax.

Clearly tea would not have been the only source of dissent at the Boston Tea Party!

Coming next time - blocks and bees ….

30

Summer Sun

Great is the sun, and wide he goes
Through empty heaven with repose;
And in the blue and glowing days
More thick than rain he showers his rays.

Though closer still the blinds we pull
To keep the shady parlour cool,
Yet he will find a chink or two
To slip his golden fingers through.

The dusty attic spider-clad
He, through the keyhole, maketh glad;
And through the broken edge of tiles
Into the laddered hay-loft smiles.

Meantime his golden face around
He bares to all the garden ground,
And sheds a warm and glittering look
Among the ivy's inmost nook.

Above the hills, along the blue,
Round the bright air with footing true,
To please the child, to paint the rose,
The gardener of the World, he goes.

Robert Louis Stephenson

Seeds for Next Summer ....

The cutting garden I established for Rosie's wedding in June has been thriving, providing me with blooms for the house the whole summer long. But as the days begin to shorten and autumn is around the corner, it's time to start thinking about letting the flowers set seed and collecting some of this harvest for use next year. Seed gathering is a lovely late summer pursuit that marks this passage into autumn and the turning of the seasons of the year.

Gathering seeds from your own flowers is also a thrifty practice, saving quite a bit of money - commercially grown seeds are expensive - and keep alive memories of particular people, events (such as Rosie's wedding) and places. I have a clump of foxgloves established from seed collected on a long-ago family holiday in Cornwall and each year when the tall purple spikes of flowers appear I'm reminded of those carefree summer days.

Over the next few weeks, look out for particularly attractive specimens whose size, colour or quantity of flowers has been noticeably superior. Instead of deadheading them to encourage more blooms, or

cutting them to bring inside, mark them with a small length of coloured thread or ribbon tied around the stem. Later on, when the seeds are fully developed and beginning to dry out, place a paper bag over the flower head, cut the stem and tie around the base with string or yarn long enough to allow you to hang it upside down in a warm dry place. When the seed-head is completely dry just shake the bag to release the seeds. Ensure it really is dry though or all your efforts will be in vain as the seeds will be likely to develop mildew or rot.

Seeds gathered in this way will need protecting from strong light and extremes of temperature. Save them in small envelopes and label them carefully - trust me - you really won't remember what they are by the time spring comes around again! You can find lots of printable seed envelopes online, or if you have children why not ask them to decorate the packets, by designing a border and/or picture for the front? Pretty packets of seeds from your garden make a lovely small gift, especially if the receiver has seen and admired your beautiful flower patch. Though they may appear small and uninteresting, those small packets of seeds contain within them all the beauty, colour and scent of summer.

Emily & Albert

Emily and her brother Albert are two of the cutest little rabbits you'll find anywhere all dressed up in their best summer clothes. They have moveable joints and shiny button noses and are surprisingly easy to make with only 4 pattern pieces for each rabbit (plus their clothes of course).

They are around 16" tall from the ends of their paws to the tips of their ears.

Not suitable for very young children due to the buttons and beads used in their construction.

You will need for one rabbit:

- 18" x 9" rabbit coloured felt
- Scraps of pale pink felt for ears
- Stranded cotton floss in colour to match rabbit coloured felt and pale pink
- Two small spherical black beads
- One small button for nose
- 4 x ¾" or 1" buttons
- Strong thread
- Toy stuffing
- 6" square cream felt for Emily
- 4" square red felt for Emily
- Red stranded floss for Emily
- 12" x 16" cotton fabric for each rabbit's clothes
- Pompoms for tails

Join pieces with wrong sides together. Use two strands of matching floss and cross stitch, working in first in one direction, then returning in the other to form a nice strong seam.

When stuffing your bunnies use small pieces of floss to avoid lumpiness and push well down into the smallest places - you will find a stuffing stick useful for this. Just take a bamboo skewer, break off the point and fray the end so it "grabs" the stuffing.

To make Arthur:

- Cut out all pieces from templates (actual size)

- Join two body pieces and stuff, then close gap as indicated on template. Join arm and leg pieces in the same way and stuff firmly. Stitch inner ears to one side of the outers, fold ears in half vertically and catch with a few stitches at the bottom edge.

- Secure arms and legs to body with strong thread. Stitch right through the body and then out through the buttons. Make a couple of passes before pulling tightly and securing end of thread behind one of the buttons.

- Stitch ears into place on the sides of the head.

- Use glass-headed pins to determine correct position of eyes. Take your time over this as their position will affect your rabbit's final expression. When you're happy stitch black beads into place with strong thread, pulling fairly tightly to add contours to the face. Add button nose and a few stitches in pale pink thread to suggest blushing cheeks.

- Add pompom tail.

To make Emily:

- Join a strip of cream felt to a strip of rabbit coloured felt by machine and press seam open. Cut out legs from this joined piece, positioning the seam where the dotted line appears on the template.

- Assemble Emily in the same way as Arthur

- Cut out two little red shoes for Emily, place on feet and join seam at front, taking a few stitches through the foot to secure in place.

Dress:

- Cut out two dress pieces from template.

- Serge or zigzag around armhole edges and finish neckhole edge.

- Join sides and hem bottom of dress.

- Slip dress onto rabbit body from the feet upwards. Slipstitch shoulder seams closed, then tuck in the armhole edges behind the tops of her arms.

- Emily is now finished.

Dungarees:

- Finish raw edges of trouser pieces, then join together along curved seam leaving gap at back for tail.

- Join legs and roll up hems. Finish top of trousers with a narrow hem.

- Hem around bib and stitch to centre front of trousers.

- Cut two 5" x ½" rectangles of fabric and fold sides to centre right side outwards. Press and top stitch by machine. Attach one short end to each top corner of the dungarees bib.

- Put dungarees on rabbit, easing tail through hole. Make pleat over tail and add an extra button to decorate if liked.

- Take straps over shoulders, crossover and tuck into back trimming length if necessary. Stitch into place

- Arthur is now finished.

Making Money from Making

I can hardly believe we've reached the end of our journey together, from the early beginnings of pricing your products, packaging and craft fairs, through branding, marketing, selling online and social media to this final chapter - setting up your own website.

Once you've started making sales through other platforms, such as Etsy, Folksy and Not on the High Street and have established your online presence through Facebook and other social media then it's time to start thinking about your own website. You can do this by having a custom-built website built to your own specific requirements (or building it yourself of course) or by using an off the peg template. Let's consider both these options ….

If you decide to have a custom-built site you'll need to purchase your domain name if you haven't already. This doesn't give you a website, but just an address or url - a "space" on the internet where your site will be.

Next you'll need to find a hosting company to give you space to host your website so you can upload all your pictures and product information so the rest of the world can see them. I'd recommend you go for at least 1 or 2 GB (gigabytes) as this will allow for future growth as your site becomes more popular.

If you're hiring a designer, then you need to think about how your website will integrate with the rest of your business - what do you want it to do for you? It's a good idea to draw a plan setting out the structure - your home page - what the other pages will be, what categories you'd like in your store, do you want to include your blog, how will people navigate around you site? This is absolutely crucial stuff - if your website isn't well thought out and properly put together then your visitors just won't stay around long enough to make a purchase.

When you're looking for a designer choose someone who's style you like and who has worked in a similar area to your own. This means they should understand your requirements, and have an awareness of your visitors' expectations too.

Your designer will want to know all about your business - however good he or she may be, they won't be a mind-reader! They may ask for a brief, or perhaps will send you a questionnaire to complete. At the least they will need:

- Business summary

- Objectives

- Business style

- Your likes and dislikes (colours, fonts, formats, illustrations etc)

- Any must-haves? (logo, branding elements etc)

- Your budget

- Time scale

It's worth running through your brief with a friend to see if they think it makes sense and if there's anything you've left out. As well as helping your designer, creating this brief will also help you clarify in your own mind exactly what you're looking for in your new website.

If all of this seems a lot of hard work, and perhaps even a little scary - then you might like to opt for a template website. These are offered by a number of companies who also offer domain registration, hosting, e-commerce and customisable design elements as part of the package. This has the advantage of being a much quicker and easier way to get started, but you may find that you're limited regarding future changes and your site may have a more generic look.

Whichever way you choose, be sure that you have the ability to update your site yourself, particularly if you'll need to add new products on a regular basis. It is very frustrating having to wait for someone to do this for you - and remember your priorities may not necessarily be theirs!

Wherever you are based in the world your website will need to be legally compliant.

You will need to:

- Clearly state your terms and conditions of trading

- Display your privacy policy - eg ask customers about accepting cookies and tell them what data collected is used for

- Protect your copyright and trademark if you have one

- Provide full contact details, including a full postal name, address and contact number. If you're a limited company then you're also required to provide the company's registered address, number and country of registration.

You'll also need to add a shopping cart to your website - or you won't be able to sell anything! Research the product that suits your business - though it's fair to say that PayPal is the market leader for small and medium sized businesses. I use PayPal here at Bustle & Sew and have found it easy to use and that it offers my customers peace of mind that their transactions will be secure.

Another advantage of PayPal is that there are no set-up charges, monthly fees or cancellation charges - you pay as you go - and fee levels are determined upon the value of your sales.

Adding a PayPal button to your site enables you to accept payment from all major credit and debit cards as well as bank accounts across the globe. You can set it up yourself in under 20 minutes.

Remember to comply with distance selling regulations. Again these will vary according to your country, but mostly they're good practice and customer service anyway.

- Offer your customers clear, concise information including details of the goods offered, delivery arrangements, cancellation rights

- Tell them about your returns and refunds policy.

And finally ….

When you're running your own business it's so easy to get wrapped up in the day to day issues, that it's easy to lose sight of your original goals. It's really important to make time to stand back and take a good look at things every so often and consider what you've achieved so far, and where you're hoping to take your business next.

Whatever challenges you're facing in your business, be confident that (almost) always there's a solution and what you're currently experiencing will have been experienced by many others before you. But, perhaps even more importantly than how the business is doing is, how are you feeling? Are you happy? Enjoying running your own business? Or do you feel stressed and miserable, dreading the day ahead? Turning your hobby into a business can be very challenging and you

shouldn't be ashamed to admit when you're feeling down about things - or even if you decide that perhaps it isn't for you after all.

Hopefully if you've been reading this series of articles from the beginning then you've found something interesting, useful or inspiring that works for you. I've tried to cover the basics - at least as I've experience them, and give you some ideas of different directions your business might take.

And to finish this series, I'm delighted to be able to tell you that my own business is taking an exciting new direction. Next month Rosie (my daughter) will be joining me here at Bustle & Sew. She's going to be managing all my social media and marketing, contributing pages to the magazine and much more too. I know she has some great new features planned for the magazine - and will be looking for contributors as well as interviewees and more too.

The Bustle & Sew website is also having a bit of an overhaul, and my little bunny is being retired and replaced by a lovely new modern version.

So watch out for next month's magazine - it's going to be better and brighter than ever!

Embroidered Floral Heart

Lovely floral heart in summer shades is a great little embroidery that fits perfectly within a 6" hoop so it's easy to stitch on the go if you choose.

I've used my finished embroidery to create a lavender heart, but you could add this design to all sorts of projects - the only limit is your imagination!

You will need:

- 7" square white or cream cotton, linen or cotton/linen blend fabric

- DMC stranded cotton floss in colours

If you are planning to make a stuffed heart like mine you will also need:

- Two x 7" squares medium weight fabric in a neutral colour(s)

- 6" x ½" wide ribbon or tape

- Stuffing - this can be lavender, toy stuffing, a mixture of both or whatever you would like to use.

- Pinking shears

Stitching Guide:

The heart is worked with two strands of floss throughout.

The only stitches used are back stitch, straight stitch and satin stitch.

To work the dual-coloured flowers begin at the centre and work straight stitches of different lengths radiating outwards from the centre, but stopping before the edges of the petals. Vary the lengths of these stitches, then fill in the space between their ends and the edges of the petals with straight stitches in the flower colour.

Finish by working a few tiny stitches at the centre to cover the place where your stitches meet.

Colour Chart

894
150
907
906
3755
745
3042
3787
Ecru

To make up heart:

- With your pinking shears cut around your embroidery ½" from the edge

- Place your heart in the centre of the right side of one of your 7" squares of background fabric and machine stitch all around the edge using matching thread.

- With right side up, fold your ribbon or tape in half and pin into place at the top of the heart, with the loop facing downwards towards the point.

- Cut out heart shape leaving a ¼" seam allowance. I find it much easier to manipulate the two squares of fabric and cut out the heart shape at the end rather than cut out two hearts first and worry about them slipping around. But that's just me. If you prefer to cut out two heart shapes and then sew them together then that's absolutely OK

- Trim seam allowances and clip curves. Turn heart the right way round and stuff. Hang by loop and enjoy!

- Pin loop into place.

- Place second 7" square of fabric on top and pin together. Flip over so the piece with the heart stitched to it is on the top.

- Usi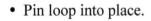hing the l arou leav

Gap for turning

Harvest Home ......

For a few days or a week or a fortnight, the fields stood 'ripe unto harvest'. It was the one perfect period in the hamlet year. The human eye loves to rest upon wide expanses of pure colour: the moors in the purple heyday of the heather, miles of green downland, and the sea when it lies calm and blue and boundless, all delight it; but to some none of these, lovely though they all are, can give the same satisfaction of spirit as acres upon acres of golden corn.

In the fields where the harvest had begun all was bustle and activity. At that time the mechanical reaper with long, red, revolving arms like windmill sails had already appeared in the locality; but it was looked upon by the men as an auxiliary, a farmers' toy; the scythe still did most of the work and they did not dream it would ever be superseded. So while the red sails revolved in one field and the youth on the driver's seat of the machine called cheerily to his horses and women followed behind to bind the corn into sheaves, in the next field a band of men would be whetting their scythes and mowing by hand as their fathers had done before them.

After the mowing and reaping and binding came the carrying, the busiest time of all. Every man and boy put his best foot forward then, for, when the corn was cut and dried it was imperative to get it stacked and thatched before the weather broke. All day and far into the twilight the yellow-and-blue painted farm wagons passed and repassed along the roads between the field and the stack-yard. Big cart-horses returning with an empty wagon were made to gallop like two-year-olds. Straws hung on the roadside hedges and many a gatepost was knocked down through hasty driving. In the fields men pitchforked the sheaves to the one who was building the load on the wagon, and the air resounded with Hold tights and Wert ups and Who-o-oas. The Hold tight! was no empty cry; sometimes, in the past, the man on top of the load had not held tight or not tight enough. There were tales of fathers and grandfathers whose necks or backs had been broken by a fall from a load, and of other fatal accidents afield, bad cuts from scythes, pitchforks passing through feet, to be followed by lockjaw, and of sunstroke; but, happily, nothing of this kind happened on that particular farm in the 'eighties.

On the morning of the harvest home dinner everybody prepared themselves for a tremendous feast, some to the extent of going without breakfast, that the appetite might not be impaired. And what a feast it was! Such a bustling in the farm-house kitchen for days beforehand; such boiling of hams and roasting of sirloins; such a stacking of plum puddings, made by the Christmas recipe; such a tapping of eighteen-gallon casks and baking of plum loaves would astonish those accustomed to the appetites of to-day. By noon the whole parish had assembled, the workers and their wives and children to feast and the sprinkling of the better-to-do to help with the serving. The only ones absent were the aged bedridden and their attendants, and to them, the next day, portions,were carried by the children from the remnants of the feast.

Long tables were laid out of doors in the shade of a barn, and soon after twelve o'clock the cottagers sat down to the good cheer, with the farmer carving at the principal table, his wife with her tea urn at another, the daughters of the house and their friends circling the tables with vegetable dishes and beer jugs, and the grandchildren, in their stiff, white, embroidered frocks, dashing hither and thither to see that everybody had what they required. As a background there was the rickyard with its new yellow stacks and, over all, the mellow sunshine of late summer.

Flora Thompson Lark Rise to Candleford

Templates

True Beauty Peacock Applique

Pattern is actual size. It is given the right way round and also reversed - to suit your preferred method of transfer and also for tracing your applique shapes onto your Bondaweb.

TRUE BEAUTY IS A Light

IN THE HEART

TRUE BEAUTY IS A Light

IN THE HEART

A Jar for Buttons

Pattern is actual size. It is given the right way round and also reversed - to suit your preferred method of transfer and also for tracing your applique shapes onto your Bondaweb.

A Jar for

Buttons

Flanders Poppies Applique

Pattern is actual size. It is given the right way round and reversed - to suit your preferred method of transfer and for tracing your applique shapes onto your Bondaweb. The three parts overlap to help you join them together.

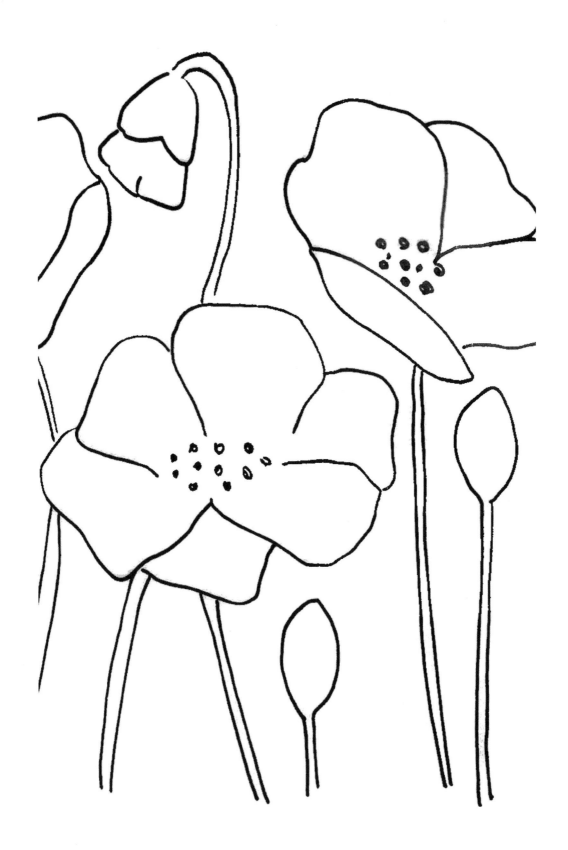

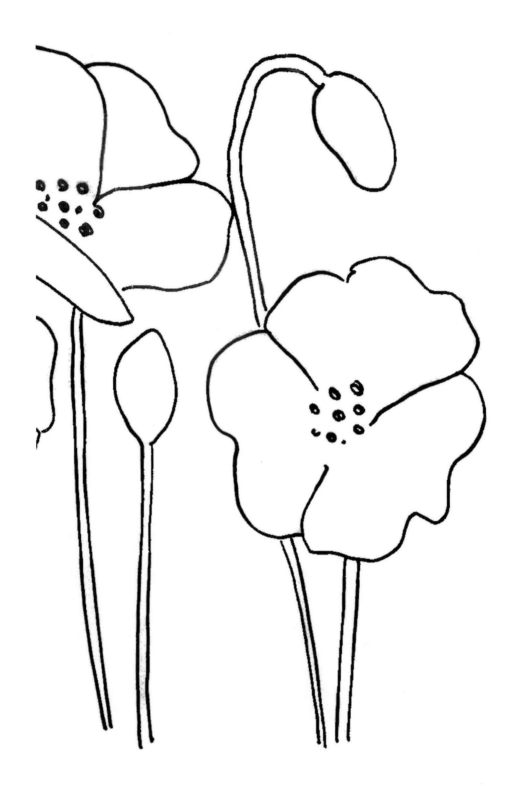

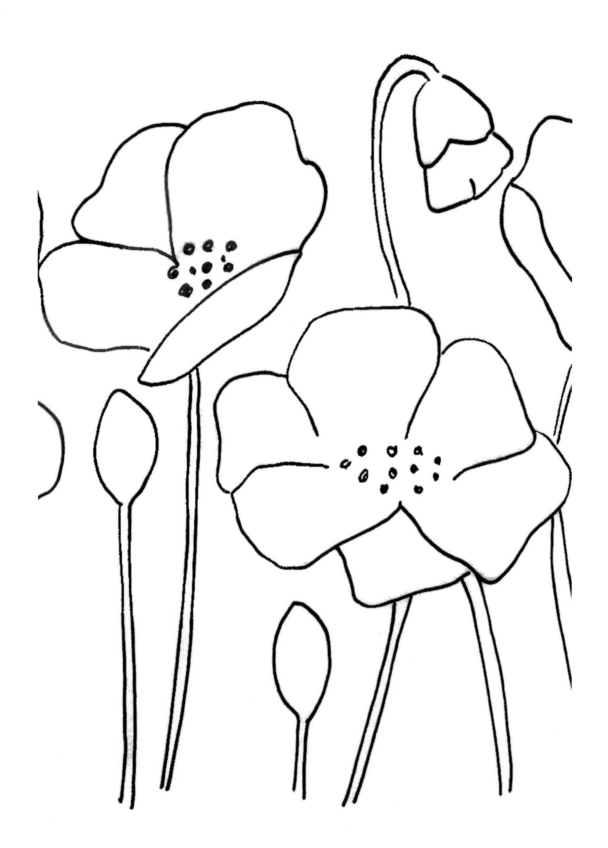

Summer Birdie Bag

Pattern is actual size. It is given reversed for tracing your applique shapes onto your Bondaweb. The two parts overlap to help you join them together.

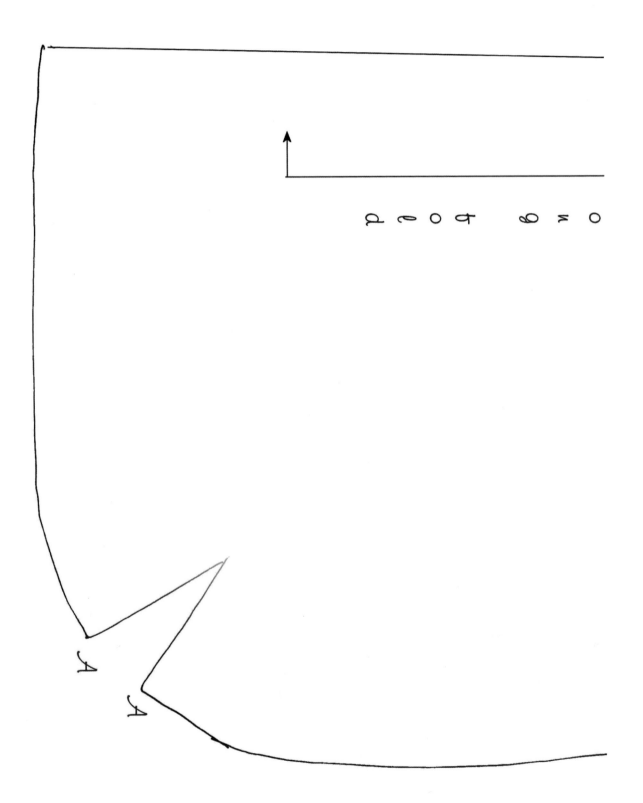

cut along edge

Main panel cut 2 in canvas and 2 in lining fabric

Emily & Albert Rabbit

Pattern is actual size.

Outer ear cut 2 rabbit colour felt

Inner ear
cut 2 pink felt

Shoe cut
2 on fold for
Fold Emily

Fold

Leg cut
4
Rabbit
colour for
Arthur
and 4 with
cream felt
on dotted line
for Emily

Body Cut 2
Rabbit Colour Felt

Leave open for stuffing

Position of
Tail

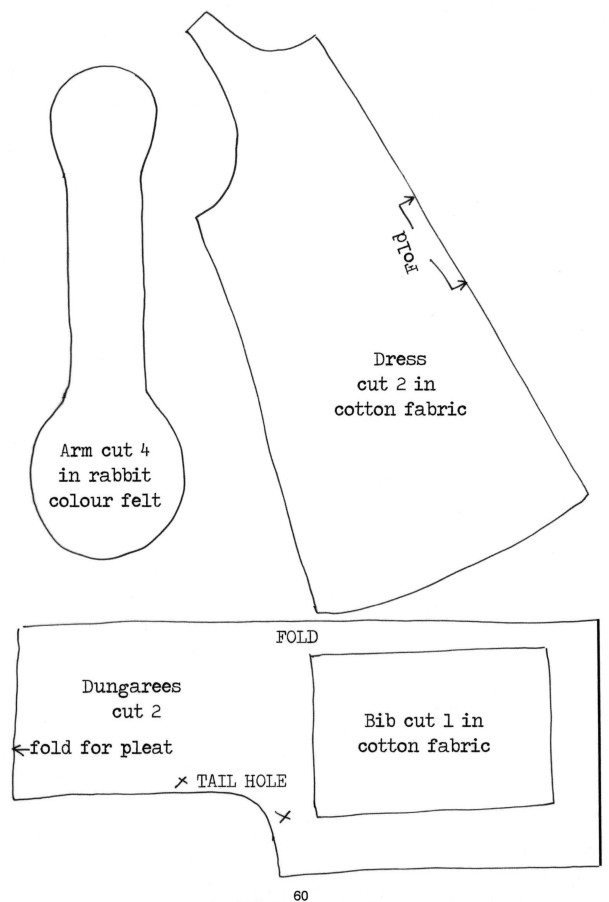

Arm cut 4
in rabbit
colour felt

Dress
cut 2 in
cotton fabric

Fold

FOLD

Dungarees
cut 2

←fold for pleat

✕ TAIL HOLE

✕

Bib cut 1 in
cotton fabric

60

Embroidered Heart

Pattern is actual size. It is given the right way round and reversed - to suit your preferred method of transfer.